12/14/01

SP

J
BIO
CORONADO
2001

WASH
3 123

D1107935

DATE DUE

Explorers & Exploration

The Travels of
Francisco de Coronado

By Deborah Crisfield
Illustrated by Patrick O'Brien

STECK-VAUGHN
ELEMENTARY · SECONDARY · ADULT · LIBRARY

A Harcourt Company

www.steck-vaughn.com

Produced by By George Productions, Inc.

ISBN 0-7398-3338-3

Printed and bound in the United States of America
10 9 8 7 6 5 4 3 2 1 W 04 03 02 01 00

Illustration Acknowledgments:
p 4, Collection of the Roswell Museum and Art Center, Gift of the Artist; pp 6, 8, 11, 19, 23, 25, 32, North Wind Picture Archives; pp14-15, The New York Public Library; p 17, 34, The Kansas State Historical Society. All other artwork is by Patrick O'Brien.

Contents

Settling in the New World

At the start of the sixteenth century, Spain had claimed more land than any other country in the world.

Christopher Columbus had reached the Americas in 1492. Other Spaniards came to the Americas soon afterward. Hernán Cortés reached Mexico in 1519. Francisco Pizarro arrived in Peru in 1531.

These men who came to the Americas during this time were called conquistadors, the Spanish word for "conqueror." The land they claimed for Spain, and the gold and other treasures they brought back, made Spain the most powerful and wealthy nation in the world.

Francisco de Coronado

It wasn't easy for a king to govern these huge lands from across an ocean. The conquistadors were men who did not take orders from anyone. Although they still reported to the King of Spain, they really just went ahead and followed their own rules.

The king needed people who would be loyal to him. So he started to appoint men he trusted as governors, or rulers, in the Americas. One of these men was named Antonio de Mendoza. The king made him the governor of New Spain, the country that is today Mexico. Mendoza brought with him a young man named Francisco Vásquez de Coronado.

Coronado was born in 1510, in Salamanca, Spain. His father was a nobleman. Francisco was not the oldest son in the family. This meant that he would not get his father's lands when his father died. He had to find another way to make money. Therefore, when Mendoza asked Coronado to go to the Americas with him in 1535, he eagerly accepted.

Francisco Pizarro was a conquistador who came to the Americas before Coronado.

Mendoza liked Coronado very much, and Francisco quickly became one of his most trusted men, even though he was quite young. By making peace with the native peoples in the area, he soon made a name for himself. He became a member of the council, or group, that helped govern Mexico City. He also became the governor's right-hand man.

Francisco married a young lady named Beatriz de Estrada. Beatriz was very rich. When Coronado married her, he also became very rich. This wealth increased his power. At the age of 28, Francisco Coronado was appointed governor of an area in Mexico called New Galicia. He had youth, good looks, money, and a beautiful woman by his side.

Coronado was born in Salamanca, Spain.

The Seven Cities of Cibola

A well-known Spanish legend tells of seven rich bishops who left Spain in the eighth century. These bishops supposedly set up seven new cities filled with riches in a place called Cíbola. Spaniards always wondered where those cities might be.

When early explorers returned with news of the Americas, people began to think that the seven cities might really exist. Every explorer was on the lookout for them.

Shortly before Coronado was appointed governor of New Galicia, a tired group of men found their way into New Spain. Among the members of the group were three Spaniards.

Spanish explorers such as this one were always on the lookout for the seven cities.

The Spaniards were Álvar Núñez Cabeza de Vaca, Alonso del Castillo, and Andres Dorantes. With them was a black man named Esteban. The men had been on an expedition, or trip, to Florida with Hernando de Soto.

As far as they knew, they were the only survivors of the expedition. They had spent years traveling westward, and almost died many times. Eventually some native people helped them. In turn, the lost Spaniards helped the natives. They helped natives who were sick by using the little medical knowledge they had. Their fame spread. As the Spaniards moved across the land, the native people welcomed them as important doctors. Finally the natives helped them return to other Spaniards.

Mendoza questioned these travelers about the lands they had crossed. None of them had seen anything like the seven cities, but the natives had told them similar stories. Mendoza was thrilled. He sent Esteban north on a scouting trip. Some native scouts and a priest named Fray Marcos traveled with him. The priest was sent on the trip to help keep peace with the natives.

Some explorers found their way to New Spain.

It didn't work. Esteban traveled about a day in front of the others. He came to a settlement of native people. He was killed there before Fray Marcos arrived. Fray Marcos went on a bit farther, but then turned back. When he arrived in New Spain, he told Mendoza that he did not see much of the settlement. He also said that he was pretty sure it was one of the rich cities for which they were searching.

This was all Mendoza needed to hear. He sent another man, Melchior Diaz, out to see if Fray Marcos's report was correct. However, Mendoza did not wait for Diaz's report. He formed an expedition to explore the territory to the north. Mendoza appointed 29-year-old Coronado to be the leader. Over two thousand people were part of this expedition northward. Soldiers made up most of the party. But there were also hundreds of

native people, and even a few women. The expedition brought a large number of livestock for food. Wagons and horses carried supplies. Coronado himself brought along 23 horses, several sets of armor for the horses, and a golden suit of armor.

The group left the city of Compostela on February 23, 1540. Several days later, Melchior Diaz returned with his report.

Coronado's expedition carried many supplies.

Off for Cíbola

The expedition began in high spirits. The Spaniards had visions of great wealth. They had heard stories of the Spanish conquistadors who had found more gold than they could ever use. Now it was their turn.

However, right from the beginning things went badly. First the expedition met some native people who were not happy to see them. Lope de Samaniego, Coronado's second in command, was killed. It was a terrible loss for Coronado and upset everyone in the expedition. A soldier named Garcia Lopez de Cardenas took over Samaniego's job.

Shortly after that, they met up with Melchior Diaz. He was returning to Compostela. His report was not good. He had found Cíbola, he said. But it was just a group of simple stone dwellings called pueblos. Although Coronado was troubled by Diaz's report, he decided not to tell anyone and to keep going. But Coronado's silence told the people what they needed to know. If it had been good news, Coronado would have shared it.

By now the people were uneasy. One of their leaders had been killed. Now they were wondering whether there were riches out there for them to find. On top of that, the land was very hilly. This made traveling difficult and slow.

Part of Coronado's army on the trail

In order to move faster, Coronado left most of the people and supplies in a town called Culiacan. He and a smaller group pushed on toward Cíbola. They traveled through what today is northern Mexico and on into Arizona. Very little food could be found, and the men were close to starving. Many horses were lost on the rugged trails. The group was becoming depressed.

Then in midsummer, the men reached the Zuni River. Across it was the land they thought was Cíbola. But it was home to the many pueblos of a group of native people called the Zuni. Today it is part of New Mexico.

Cíbola was not what the Spaniards had imagined. Instead of seeing a great city glittering with gold and jewels, they saw a pueblo village called Hawikuh. The houses sat on top of each other and were made of roughly cut stone blocks. There were no jewels, no gold.

Coronado was disappointed, but he still had a job to do. He stepped forward to tell the native people that they were now under Spain's rule. In response, the natives attacked. They shot arrows out the windows of their houses every time Coronado tried to come closer. He finally gave the signal for his men to shoot back.

A Zuni pueblo village

The battle that followed was a fierce one. The Spaniards were hungry, angry, and disappointed. They took all this out on the natives. The natives fought bravely, but they were outmatched. They turned their attention to Coronado. In his golden armor, he was clearly the leader of the army. They threw rocks at him, and knocked him unconscious. Coronado most likely would have been killed if Cardenas and another man named Hernando de Alvarado had not dragged him to safety.

When Coronado awoke, he learned that his army had won. The natives had fled their town. The Spaniards were feasting on all the food they could find. The fight had lasted an hour.

Exploring More Places

Coronado and his men settled into the town of Hawikuh. They made peace with the Zuni, and many of these natives returned to live in the city with the Spaniards.

Now it was time for some more explorations. This time, Coronado sent out small groups rather than the whole army. The first thing he did was to send a few men, including Fray Marcos, back to Mexico City to tell Mendoza that Hawikuh was not one of the seven cities of gold. Then he sent Melchior Diaz back to the rest of the army to tell them to join him in Hawikuh. Diaz was also told to explore the lands to the west. He became the first European to set foot in California.

It was late July when the first scouting mission set off. They were under the command of a soldier named Pedro de Tovar. They headed to the northwest, into what we call Arizona.

Tovar's group came across a tribe of native people called the Hopi. Like the Zuni, the Hopi didn't have any riches. They welcomed the Spaniards into their city. Later, when the Spaniards refused to leave the city, a fight broke out. It didn't last long. As soon as the Hopi saw the Spaniards' swords, they surrendered.

The Hopi were unable to tell the Spaniards about a city of gold, but they did tell them about a great canyon to the west, with a huge river running through it.

Tovar decided that this information was worth passing on to Coronado. He sent word back, and soon Coronado organized a second group of men. The leader of this expedition was Cardenas, Coronado's second in command and one of the men who had saved his life during the battle at Hawikuh.

Cardenas knew he was searching for a great river that cut through a deep canyon. However, he wasn't prepared for the spectacular sight he and his party saw. They were the first Europeans to set eyes on the Grand Canyon.

A distant view of a Hopi city

Even after they saw this huge natural wonder, they didn't believe that the canyon was as deep as their native guides said it was. And the river could not be a great river. They could barely see it. How could it be huge?

Cardenas sent a few men down into the canyon. After climbing for most of the day, the men weren't even halfway down. Cardenas called them back. At that point he had to admit to the natives that the canyon was much bigger than it appeared. In fact, the men spent three days trying to get down to the river but never made it.

While Cardenas and Tovar were away on their expeditions in Arizona, some native people from a tribe to the east came to visit the strange new men who had come to their land. They came in peace.

The chief had a big mustache. The explorers called him Bigotes, which means "whiskers" in Spanish. Bigotes told Coronado that he and his men were welcome, as long as they came in peace. Bigotes said they came from a village in the east called Cicuye. It was on the banks of a great river, which was later called the Rio Grande.

The Grand Canyon—Cardenas and his men were the first Europeans to see it.

Bigotes said he would help the Spaniards make peace with the many other native peoples who lived along the river.

Coronado appreciated the help that Bigotes gave him. He also liked and respected the chief, and treated him as a friend.

Bigotes described fertile lands to the east that were covered by huge herds of buffalo. Cabeza de Vaca, one of the men who had wandered into New Spain shortly before Coronado's expedition began, had talked of these strange animals, too.

Because Coronado trusted Bigotes, he decided to send a third scouting party to the east. Coronado felt that if there was any hope of finding the golden cities, it was probably in that direction. Coronado appointed Alvarado, the other man who had saved his life, as leader of this third party.

Again, the search proved to be disappointing. Alvarado did find buffalo and very fertile land, but no gold. He sent word back to Coronado, suggesting that the army move eastward for the winter. He also suggested that they settle in the villages of a group of native people called the Tiguex, who lived along the Rio Grande.

Each time a scouting party went out, Coronado was hopeful for reports of gold. On the other hand, he was not surprised when there weren't any. In a letter he wrote to Mendoza, he said that the mission to find the lost cities was unlikely to succeed. But he hadn't given up completely, and would still explore the territory for Spain. At this point, Coronado had to choose. He was fascinated by the description of the Grand Canyon in the west. However, he felt that the fertile land to the east was a better choice.

Bigotes spoke of herds of buffalo, which Coronado and his men had never seen before.

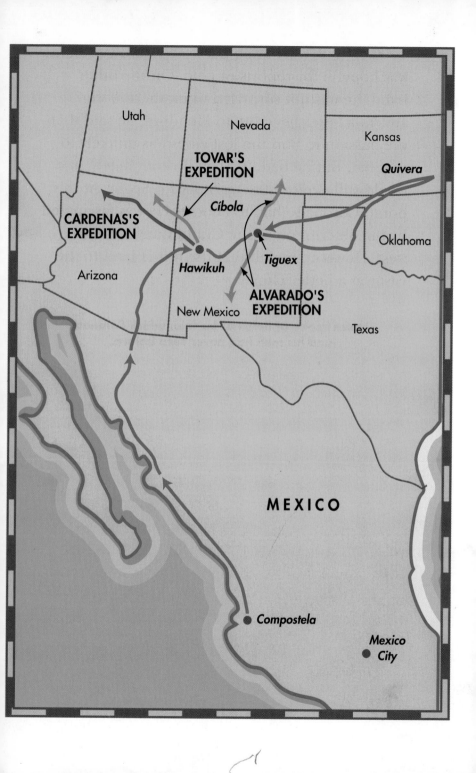

The End of Peace

Most of Coronado's army reached Hawikuh in November. They were cold, hungry, and tired. Because of this, Coronado didn't leave for Tiguex immediately. Instead, he sent Cardenas ahead with a smaller group to set up camp. Cardenas decided that the army would take over the southernmost village, and he ordered the natives living there to move out.

Meanwhile, Alvarado had taken his group to Bigotes's land of Cicuye. He and his men were welcomed, as the native chief had said they would be. Alvarado tried to convince Bigotes to join their expedition even further eastward, but Bigotes felt that he could not be away from his people for such a long time. In his place he sent two captured members of another tribe to act as guides. One was named Sopete. The Spaniards called the other one El Turco (The Turk) because he wore a turban on his head.

The Turk had no loyalty either to Bigotes or to the Spaniards. He decided to use the Spaniards to help him get back to his people. He told them that the cities for which they were searching lay in the east, in a place called Quivera. He said that in Quivera, gold was everywhere. Even the pots and pans were made of gold.

The Spaniards were excited. Finally they were getting close to the riches they had hoped for. The Turk's tales became more elaborate. He said he would have had proof but Bigotes had stolen his golden bracelets when he was captured.

Instead of going on to Quivera, Alvarado and his group went back to Bigotes to get proof. They demanded to see the bracelets. Bigotes laughed at them and told them that the Turk was a liar. He never had any gold bracelets and there was no gold in Quivera. The place only had a lot of grass huts.

Even though they didn't get the proof they were looking for, the Spaniards believed the Turk's stories. And they ignored the words of their trusted friend. They were that eager for gold.

The Spaniards trusted the Turk, but he always led them astray.

The Spaniards put chains on Bigotes and took him back to Tiguex with them to discuss the situation with Coronado.

In Tiguex, things were not going well. Coronado had arrived with the entire army. It was cold and there was not enough room or supplies for all of them. The soldiers were stealing blankets, food, and clothing from the villages. In turn, the native people killed some of the Spaniards' horses. Cardenas was furious, and Coronado gave him permission to punish the natives.

But Coronado did not know what Cardenas had in mind. Cardenas and his men killed at least 30 of the native people. When Coronado found out about this, he was horrified. But he did not punish

A battle between the Spaniards and the native people.

Cardenas. Besides, now peace with the natives was at an end. The two groups hated each other.

Shortly after that, Alvarado arrived with Bigotes in chains. Seeing a chief being treated in such a way angered the Tiguex even more. To show the natives that he was right to have chained Bigotes, Coronado wanted to prove that the chief was a liar. He tried to force Bigotes to "tell the truth." But Bigotes stuck to his story.

Now the Tiguex rebelled. Fighting began. When they realized they were outnumbered, the natives retreated to their best-protected village, the Moho pueblo. Coronado decided to starve them out. After a winter with little food, the Tiguex surrendered. The Spanish killed many of them.

Coronado's army heads to Quivera.

Following the Turk

In spring 1541 Coronado and his army headed east to the city of Quivera. Coronado's army numbered about 1,500 at this point. As they neared Cicuye, Coronado set Bigotes free.

The Turk led the way. While the men did come upon huge herds of buffalo, they found little else. The other guide, Sopete, kept telling the Spaniards not to trust the Turk. He told them that the Turk was leading them south, away from Quivera. He was right. The Spaniards had just been wandering all around what is now called Texas, while Quivera is in present-day Kansas.

Finally Coronado believed Sopete and put the Turk in chains. The native admitted that he had been trying to get them lost. At this point, Coronado realized that the Turk had been lying to them all along. He sent most of his army back to Tiguex. He continued forward with a small group. Sopete was now in the lead.

When they came to Quivera, they saw that it was nothing like the place that the Turk had described. In fact, Bigotes had told the truth. Quivera only had a lot of grass huts. Quivera did have rich land for farming, however, and Coronado claimed it for Spain. Today we call it Kansas, and it still has rich farmland.

The scouting party stayed in Quivera for about a month. At first the native people were friendly, but that soon changed because the Turk had been spreading lies about the Spaniards. Coronado decided that it was time to leave.

Many of the men with Coronado wanted to stay in Quivera. It had the richest farmland they'd ever seen, and they hoped to become rich landowners. Coronado promised them that the expedition would come back, but first he wanted them to rejoin the rest of the army in Tiguex. So they all headed westward, settling in for the winter in Tiguex once again.

Then, in December of 1541, Coronado had a terrible accident. While he was horse racing for fun, a strap broke and his saddle slipped off the horse. As Coronado fell to the ground, the horse kicked him in the head. The explorer hung between life and death for days.

Although Coronado recovered, he wasn't the same man. Before the accident, the explorer was a great and respected leader. Now Coronado was a weak, injured man who just wanted to go home to see his wife.

Coronado's Return

Coronado told the army of his change in plans. They were all going back to Mexico instead of back to Quivera. Many of the men were furious. They had come to the Americas to find gold and land. There was no gold, but there was plenty of land. Yet Coronado was forcing them to stay in the army and return to Mexico City. It was an angry army that followed their injured leader southward in 1542.

It was a difficult trip back over the rough ground. Three months and 900 miles (1,448 km) later, they entered Culiacan, the northernmost city in New Spain.

Most of the army were discharged, or released from service, at this point. Lying on a stretcher, Coronado continued on to Mexico City with fewer than 100 men. It was not the successful return he had imagined.

Coronado before he became a sickly man.

Coronado returned to Mexico City on a stretcher.

Coronado's misery didn't end there. He was put on trial for the crimes he had committed against the native peoples. Mendoza supported Coronado, and the judge eventually decided he was innocent. However, Cardenas was sentenced to seven years in jail for killing the 30 Tiguex.

Coronado lived the rest of his life fairly quietly. He took a position on the city council, but he was mostly a private man. He never again set out on an expedition. He died 12 years later, in 1544, at the age of 44.

Coronado always thought that his expedition was a failure. And for centuries, so did other people. But he had reached more places than almost everyone else before him. He explored the present-day states of California, Arizona, New Mexico, Texas, Oklahoma, and Kansas. His soldiers were the first Europeans to see the Grand Canyon, the Colorado River, and the Rio Grande. Today he is known as the first European to reach the southwestern part of the United States.

Other Events of the 16th Century
(1501 – 1600)

During the century that Coronado was exploring, events were happening in other parts of the world. Some of these were:

1502   Portuguese navigator Vasco da Gama makes his second voyage to India in order to expand trade.

1521   Hernán Cortés, a Spanish conquistador, conquers the Aztec Empire in Mexico.

1524   Giovanni da Verrazano, an Italian sailor, explores the coast of North America from North Carolina to Maine.

1534   Francisco Pizarro of Spain conquers the Inca Empire in Peru.

1571   Portuguese create colony of Angola, Africa.

1578   Moroccans destroy Portuguese power in northwest Africa.

Time Line

1510	Coronado is born in Salamanca, Spain.
1535	Coronado goes to the Americas with Mendoza.
1536	Cabeza de Vaca comes to New Spain and tells of his trip across the continent.
1538	Coronado is appointed governor of New Galicia.
1539	Esteban and Fray Marcos begin a scouting mission to Cíbola.
1539	Fray Marcos returns with stories of riches; Diaz is sent out to confirm this.
1540	Coronado is appointed leader of the expedition, which departs February 23.
March 1540	Melchior Diaz gives Coronado his discouraging report.
July 1540	Coronado reaches Cíbola and the battle of Hawikuh follows.
July 1540	Tovar is sent out with a scouting party and comes upon the Hopi tribe.
August 1540	Cardenas sets out and later reaches the Grand Canyon.
August 1540	Bigotes arrives in camp.
August 1540	Alvarado and Bigotes head east to the Rio Grande.

September 1540	The Turk and Sopete join the expedition.
November 1540	The rest of the army reaches Cíbola.
November 1540	Cardenas sets up camp in Tiguex.
December 1540	Coronado and the rest of the army arrive in Tiguex.
December 1540	Bigotes arrives in chains.
December 1540	The battle of Moho begins.
spring 1541	The natives at Moho surrender.
spring 1541	The Turk leads the Spaniards all over present-day Texas.
summer 1541	Coronado sends most of his army back to Tiguex and goes on to Quivera.
fall 1541	Coronado returns to Tiguex.
December 1541	Coronado falls from his horse and is kicked in the head.
spring 1542	The army begins the journey back to New Spain.
1544	Coronado and Cardenas are put on trial for their actions at Tiguex. Coronado is freed, but Cardenas is sentenced to seven years in prison.
1554	Coronado dies.

Glossary

canyon (KAN-yun) A deep and narrow valley with high sides

Cíbola (SEE-bow-luh) The area in present-day New Mexico where early Spanish explorers thought the legendary seven golden cities were located. Instead they found the pueblo villages of the Zuni.

conquistador (kon-KEES-tuh-dor) The Spanish word for "conqueror," or leader in the Spanish conquest of the Americas in the 1500s

expedition (ek-spuh-DISH-un) A journey for a special purpose, such as to explore or take over lands

fray (FRAY) The Spanish word for a priest

governor (GUV-ur-nur) The name given to the ruler or leader of an area or a group of people

Grand Canyon A gigantic valley that cuts through present-day Arizona. It was formed by the Colorado River and the shifting of the earth's crust.

Hawikuh (HUH-wi-kuh) One of the Zuni pueblos in Cíbola and site of a battle between the Zuni and Coronado's army.

Hopi (HO-peeh) A tribe of Native Americans from present-day Arizona

Moho (MOW-hoh) The best-protected village of the Tiguex tribe during Coronado's time

New Galicia (guh-LEE-syuh) The Spanish name for an area in western Mexico during Coronado's time

pueblo (poo-EB-low) A village of Native Americans of the American southwest. The dwellings are made of mud and bricks, and are stacked on top of one another

Quiverans (KEEVEE-runs) A tribe of Native Americans from present-day Kansas

Rio Grande (REE-oh GRAND-ee) A long river that flows from a mountain in Colorado to the Gulf of Mexico

Tiguex (TIG-oh) A tribe of Native Americans from present-day Texas

Zuni (ZOO-nee) A tribe of Native Americans from present-day New Mexico

Index